Sentient Understanding

Mastering One's Demons

Edward L. Hannon

Content

Foreword

This book has symbolically and esoterically 5,121 words; which marks a definitive end, but, also a new beginning. For, in order to master one's demons, and then transcend them, it requires openness, understanding and an honest acceptance of "The Self;" which, in essence, is the eternal and absolute nature of the, "I AM THAT I AM." For within this understanding, one may find that the ultimate reality of truth is that one is fundamentally boundless; thus, one must seek to discipline this limitless disposition, through a stalwart compass of principled direction. Thereby, one can know that through acceptance, wisdom patiently awaits to offer its profound harvest of negotiable resilience.

Acknowledgement

I dedicate this book to The OMNI, TAO, SOURCE, THE SINGULARITY, The GOD-FACTOR, and/or The "I AM THAT I AM;" which is essentially ALL there IS; especially, the mentality of Man/Woman, Being ITS most basic, yet unrealized state.

Philosychology

Philosychology (noun) is a study of conscious behavior created by PhTCB (philosopher and teacher of conscious behavior) Edward L. Hannon. This science is a synthesis of empirical psychology along with his philosophies to methodize a practical or practicable solution to resolve the dilemmas, conflicts, or queries that mankind perpetuates upon itself.

I have spoken with one tongue, which knows every voice; and, I have performed with one purpose, that knows every struggle. For, I AM light, which recognizes myself, even being within the pitch of utter darkness; because, I shine unabated, regardless of its inducing shadows of insubstantial fear.

Time, is but a form of light; for it emits the premise of shadows, by which, we dividedly rationalize the significance of moments.

I saw you with an eye, which would only accept the depths of reason; thus, I chose to become blind to that which my eyes could embrace to be totally superficial.

A fragile mentality must boast about having power; but, a poised disposition explains what it means to be in true power.

As subtle as a wick that fuels the nature of the flame, inspiration remains ever content to reinforcibly dance within the passion of the fire.

Diplomacy, can be explained as the art of entertaining, accepting and then finding the proper context of that which would otherwise be dismissed as unfathomable

Dark souls fear the essence of true light; for they intrinsically know that its radiance emits a responsibility, by which, they must encounter change, if they are to develop any further.

The grace of understanding burns intensely for those that would be good stewards of their ears to prudently listen.

If a withered leaf can be retained by a branch, until, it is removed by the wind, than how much more can we lend the arm of support to another; until, they firmly decide to let go, to be carried away by the whispers of others?

The passion of togetherness, whether being large and small, or the greatest and the least, must strive in unison; in order to eventually meet the productive expectations of cooperation.

As the flame speaks in dance, silent are my gazing eyes; for they are symbolically witnessing that which offers success to a vision.

I speak with a voice, which audibly cannot be heard; but, ever yearns to be understood, for I AM the silent tongue of the mind.

As a candle is extinguished, and can be revived by a spark; so does the mortal vessel sleeps and rises, until, it truly awakens to become an existential capacitor of endless possibility.

It has been said that, in order to win every war do not enter a battle, which cannot be won; therefore, do not try to control that which you cannot begin to manage.

Time can speak through the essence of shadows. Time can speak through the expressions of the seasons; and time can speak through the voice of experience. But, do you have a mind that is intuitive enough to listen?

"YOU," that is NAMELESS has lit me; thus, I have become the Divine spark of but One IDENTITY, which is the "I AM" of absolute potential.

How can we recognize those who are unjust? The answer is simple, for you will witness them running from ill-intended shadows, which resemble their own.

I left a place; which, I inherently know that I can never leave. For here, there is an indelible sense of knowing that I can never truly escape that which I absolutely am. So, my attempted departure was but a jaunt of psychologically shuffling through, and then reaffirming the boundless aspects of my total sense of being.

Minds that are bound to egotistical behavior are as one locked within a prison; for they sentence themselves to a precarious state, to where they can remain an ever captive of their foolish pride.

Jealous souls, which in a colloquial sense may be called a hater, possess minds that are devoid of passion. So, in frustration, they seethe with resentment; thus, becoming as a vampire to feed off of others creativity.

Solitude, does not beg, nor shun the presence of friendship; for, it endeavors to understand the motives of those who profess to call themselves a friend, lest ignorance would inadvertently birth an enemy.

Love is a language, which does not have to speak. Love is an idea, which is known; therefore, does not have to be explained. Love is intangible; unless, it is made substantial through understanding. Subsequently, love can be fashioned out of nothing at all.

Never devote your life to feeling as though you have to become the opinion of what others may think of you.

After feeling as though they have lost all control, dispossessed mentalities will total disable their entire sense of well-being, by abandoning all personal values; which leaves their state to be irresolutely devoid of any hope of finding constitution.

What is the nature of a true psychological magician? Answer: It is one that resiliently maximizes the minimum, thereby, becoming as a chameleon or a shapeshifter, whereas others may succumb to failure by exhibiting an inflexible ego.

Why would a fool attempt to shine a light, within the brightness of day? Answer: Because, contrary to the environment, it overwhelmingly knows that its mentality is walking in utter darkness.

I AM a friend to all; for the only enemy that I see is division. Therefore, I intrinsically know that I must never settle for a state that would willfully promote strife.

In my final analysis, within this realm of life, I have learned to appreciate, understand and accept another's opinion, without feeling as though it is my responsibility to change them.

I have finally arrived at a location; which has no definitive destination. Thus, I AM now free to remain ever content in being here.

Existentialism

Existential Contradistinction

If GOD, SOURCE, TAO, UNIVERSE or THE SINGULARITY is ONE, then why would IT, Intelligently Design ITSELF to house the emotive quality or stance of resistance within ITSELF? My answer would be to consider a "Viva voce," which is one of the final phrases of a doctoral program; whereby, the aspirant(s) must meet with the respective internal and external (control and variable) experts within their chosen field of study, in order to reasonably and/or authentically assert, and then defend the thesis (premise) of their claim. For, as it has been said, in the Hermetic principles: "As above, so below, as within, so without, as with the Universe, so is the soul."

Dark Theological Existentialism: Concept

Nihilist: "Why are we here?"

Spiritualist: "First, explain to me, what and where is the nature of here?/."

Nihilist: "What, I mean by here, is this place we call life."

Spiritualist: "You appear to be here, thus, you have experienced that which you have questioned for quite some time."

Nihilist: "Yes, what is your point?"

Spiritualist: "You have adapted well to that which you may feel is meaningless, useless and/or without purpose. So, what, makes you participate, therefore, what, could be the point./?"

Orb Manifestations: Existential Concept

I have, on occasion, had the momentous experience of witnessing light-orb anomalies; within a photographic lens or frame of a space. These orbs, although quite translucent, had very little mass and varying degrees of illumination; and, I also noticed that they seem to move, in accordance, with the cognizant of a perspective environment. Therefore, by that experience, I AM of the premise to assert that light-orb anomalies are clear indications that existence-itself is fundamentally kaleidoscopic or dimensionally multi-layered within frequencies; which, by perception, it individually offers a dynamic sensory induced approach of physiologically exploring, knowing and/or defining, the intimate features of itself, being indelibly only a singular essence.

Relationship Objective Concept:

We are One; but, paradoxically, not necessarily the same. So, please allow me to be a pupil of your ways that I may study, learn and know who you truly are.

Telekinetic Photonic Interplay: Concept

Electromagnetic fusion, as it relates to the Hermetic principles, can be defined as sensory positioning and/or trans-positioning; in order to facilitate interpersonal expressions and transactions between categorically charged energy potential. Therefore, existence-itself, being not fundamentally distinct to be considered solely a physical property, behaves to induce a psychosomatic fashion of structural experience; through that which is known in the Hermetic principles as vibration.

Esoteric/Occult Mysteries

In an acronymic sense, I have learned to accept and embrace existence, with an unbounded "L.U.S.T.;" which can be feasibly articulated in the reality of love, understanding, sapience and truth.

Theological/Occult Concept:

Language can be the marriage of religion, culture and ideas: for example: "The word, Frau, in German, has been defined, as a formal title for a married woman." Next, let us consider the idea or concept of "Chaos;" for in some ancient cultures, chaos was perceived as sometimes equally necessary, just as the reality of order. Thereby, one could discern that the marriage of extremes or differences may help expand existential ideas; for instances: within the words, "In Frau Chaos," one can unravel the words and the cultural school of thought of, "Africa Oshun."

Luminous Paradox:

I AM light, which through dance, may express the mood of an environment. For, I can confirm the nature of Newtonian physics, while yet, at times, be in direct defiance of them; because, I AM also the illumination, which can explain the quantum nature of ether; by the simple presentation of one observing me as the flame of a candle.

Psychological Warfare Concept: Two Potential Adversaries

Incontestable warrior: "I have never loss an engagement; therefore, I will never fall prey to failure. So, how do you think that you can ever have a tactical advantage over me?"

Shapeshifting warrior: "I would first give you the high ground of exposing your mental potential; by which, you already have. And, if, by some chance, we must engage, I know that I am no stranger to failure; for it has yielded me some of the most prudent lessons. Whereby, I had to relinquish my pride; lest I would be fit only to be its most redundant student."

As the radius of time's wisdom increases, the necessity of change, whether environmentally and/or psychologically, must be ever adjusted; in order to accommodate for a more evolved approach, lest, cryptically, a "Radial Turn as Set" completely voids the functionality within a society.

As with the Tetragrammaton (YHVH) of ages before, men who were ignorant of their personal Divine Identity, tried to capture and harness the ineffable name of GOD; so, as a new age dawns, here is a Pentagrammaton (MA-I-TAHT-I-AM), to prudentially reminder us all of our eternally Olden Identity.

Redeemed Apostasy

I do not be(lie)ve in GOD; because, I have learned to study myself, in order to know GOD from within. On this path, I have also learned the bygone art of what others may pejoratively call witchcraft, but, which I see and phrase as existential synchronicity; for, as we endeavor to understand the nature of the stars and heaven (thought), then the earth (body) must be beholden to its every precept. So, we may strive to be in ever accordance, with the indelible birthright of our Divinely Immortal IDENTITY.

Ξ

Please remember to:

(1-12-23-1-25-19) (2-5) (7-18-1-20-5-6-21-12)

Ξ

It has been real, but:

(7-15-15-4-2-25-5) (11-1-12-9) (25-21-7-1)

Ξ

The Elucidation of Immaculate Conception

If we consider the first Hermetic principle of mentalism, which states that ALL is Mind, and further reflect that ALL is essentially One, then fundamentally there is no such state of perfection, nor imperfection. But, if we realize that every thought, plan, goal or objective is an ideal or concept of the mind; then each and every ideation must be considered immaculate, by virtue of their very nature. For there is nothing that can be envisioned, whether good, bad and/or indifferent, which lack an immaculate concept of some sort of idyllic fulfillment; because no one ever truly endeavors in a conception, with a deliberate aim or goal of seeking failure; no matter great, mediocre or disastrous. Thus, thought-itself always carries the immaculacy of a desired state and/or reality.

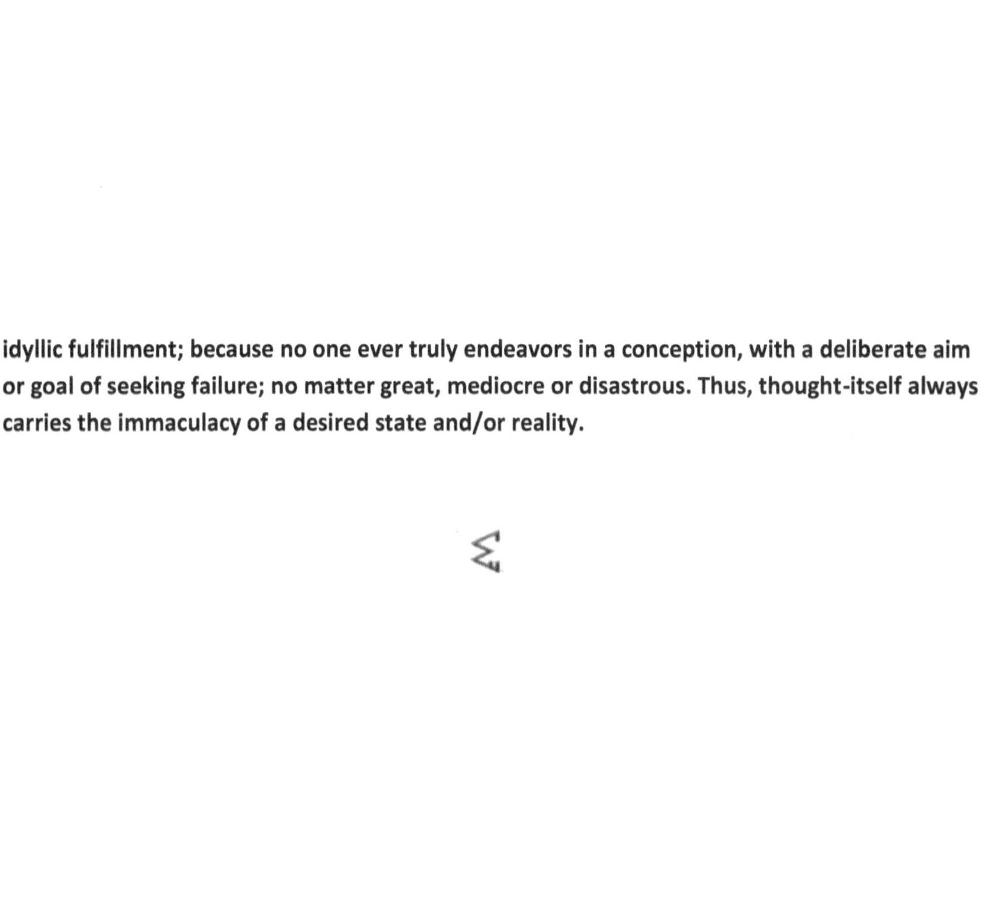

Dark Psychological Humor

Dark and Morbid Theological Humor: An Incorrigible Sinner

Sinner: "Priest, I have sinned."

Priest: "No problem, just recite a few chants and take these holy beads, then try to not sin anymore."

Sinner: "I cannot in good conscience."

Priest: "Why?"

Sinner: "Because, where I would creatively want to put them, could be the origin of a new sin."

Dark Theological Humor:

Demons: "We need your help."

Angels: "How may we be of assistance?"

Demons: "We want to peer into the heart, soul and mind of man; without violating their privacy, for we understand the rules of engagement."

Angels: "Have you all considered the golden rule, which is: "Do unto others, as you would have them do unto you?"

Demons: "That is a perfect pretext, thus, we can use it to temporarily relinquish our powers to man; thus, as we uninhibitedly expose who we are, by being willing to be an example, once our powers return, man's psychology will be totally incapacitated; for, we shall be able to predict, and then thwart their every move."

Dark Theological/Occult Humor:

Cathar: "YAHWEH, how will I know that YOU have released me from this mortal time-oriented bodily prison?"

YAHWEH: "Because, you are, in essence, categorically energy-charged potential, which cannot be created, nor destroyed. Thus, once your mortal sentence is complete, your mortal remains become an ever reminder that all charges were dropped."

Dark Theological Humor:

Parishioner: "Satan, give me a reason why I should never engage with You."

Satan: "Because, you may not intrinsically understand why I AM always welcoming."

Dark Theological Humor:

Friend one: "Why do you continuously allow yourself to be manipulated by trying to please people?"

Friend two: "It is a psychological sharpening tactic; which I like to call the serpent."

Friend one: "Please explain."

Friend two: "Once you endeavor to be kind, peaceful and accepting of people, from all walks of life, especially when you are jilted, on occasion, by hostility, you realize the caliber of their psychological worth. Because they cannot help, but reveal that which they are fundamentally made of."

Friend one: "Then, what do you do?"

Friend two: "I may see it fit to become calculating and ruthlessly detached."

Friend one: "Isn't that a bit sinister?"

Friend two: "Not if you understand the occult and Biblical passage, which says: "Be ye wise as serpents, and harmless as a dove."

Dark Humor:

Friend one: "Don't be manipulated."

Friend two: "Why would you say that?"

Friend one: "Because, you are too loving, and others may see that as a weakness."

Friend two: "Would you say that manipulation has a purpose?"

Friend one: "Yes of course, or it would not exist."

Friend two: "Would you also say that unconditionally love has a hidden agenda or purpose?"

Friend one: "No, it is without guile and glaringly transparent."

Friend two: "So, how could I ever be manipulated by that which may have a purpose, but lacks the stability of understanding? For, I, myself, remain ever enraptured by a foundational nonlocality of existential acceptance and causality; which incessantly births what can be the ephemeral identity, agenda and qualitative experience of purpose-itself."

Dark Theological Humor:

Investor: "I am a skilled investor, who believes in investing in only sure endeavors; for you only get one chance to live."

Monk: "Did you have an investing mentor, before you started investing?"

Investor: "Yes, why do you ask?"

Monk: "They must have been quite convincing, to not only get you to invest in something that you cannot take with you to the grave, but, to do it with such alacrity, for ultimately knowing that your fate was already dismally sealed."

Dark Theological Humor:

Pupil: "Master, I have been under your tutelage for years, and I don't understand why I have not become enlightened."

Zen Master: "Perhaps, you are not seeking to understand that which offers purpose to the concept of light-itself."

Pupil: "Which is?"

Zen Master: "The inquisitiveness of who, what, where, when, how and why of utter darkness."

Dark Humor: Relationship Perils

Spouse one: "I will only break your heart."

Spouse two: "Do not flatter yourself, because that which you speak of, is an ignorant tardiness of what could have been the fate of a long departed, yet hopelessly romantic simpleton; but, those words, as of late, can be essential for seducing the nonnegotiable stoicism of a potential monster."

Dark Humor:

Spouse one: "Baby, you are stoic, thus hardly apt to show feelings; but, you may not be as intelligent as me. Because there is this study, which states that intelligent people, as myself, are prone to sleep on their back; while emotional people tend to sleep on their side."

Spouse two: "Will you please excuse me, as I fluff my pillow and turn to my side, in order to get some sleep?"

Spouse one: "Did you hear anything that I said?"

Spouse two: "Yes, I am just about to get in touch with my feelings."

Dark Humor: Interment Arrangement

Spouse one: "Baby, sorry to hear about the loss of your friend."

Spouse two: "Thank you, but we were not as close as we once were; besides, he owed me a substantial amount of money, and I heard that he died penniless."

Spouse one: "Baby, you do not have to be so heartless; for you can at least pay your last respects, by giving one of your suits to bury him in."

Spouse two: "Okay, fine, I will let you pick one out."

Spouse one: "Wow, baby, I am so proud of you; because, I noticed that after the last viewing, you finally became emotional and overcome in grief."

Spouse two: "Yes, I did, because once they closed the casket, I knew that it would be the last time, I would see, and much less have the opportunity to wear, one of my favorite suits."

Σ

Dark Humor:

Stranger one: "Are you good?"

Stranger two: "I would say that I AM balanced and just; but, if I AM considered good, it is by default."

Stranger one: "Please explain."

Stranger two: "If someone were to ask me, would I sell my soul for all the trappings of fame and success, I would be inclined to say, nah I AM good."

Σ

Dark Theological Humor:

Friend one: "I heard that you were excommunicated because of your spiritual convictions. Are you willing to make any changes?"

Friend two: "Yes, perhaps, the time that I usually go to bed."

Σ

Dark Theological Humor:

Demons: "GOD, please forgive us for breaking rank; but, since Satan is away traveling to and fro, we need YOUR help to resolve the ever growing issue of man's recklessly materialistic mentality. Which of us demons do YOU feel is more suited to deal with such worthlessness?

GOD: "Belial."

Dark Theological Humor:

Stranger one: "Who, in the hell do you think that you are, to show up, at such, an opulently formal event in mere rags?"

Stranger two: "The chosen of GOD, for such an event, but you can just call me, Belial."

Dark Humor:

Friend one: "How do you or could you just venture into places, where people are hateful, hostile, abusive, evil and outright dangerous?"

Friend two: "Simply, because you are fearful, and assume that you and I are positioned at the same psychological state. "

Dark Humor:

Friend one: "What do you do when malignant people feel compelled to constantly remind you of your past; especially, after you have made definite strides to profoundly change?"

Friend two: "Smile, for this may be their only sense of hope, which they can expect to see in their far distant future."

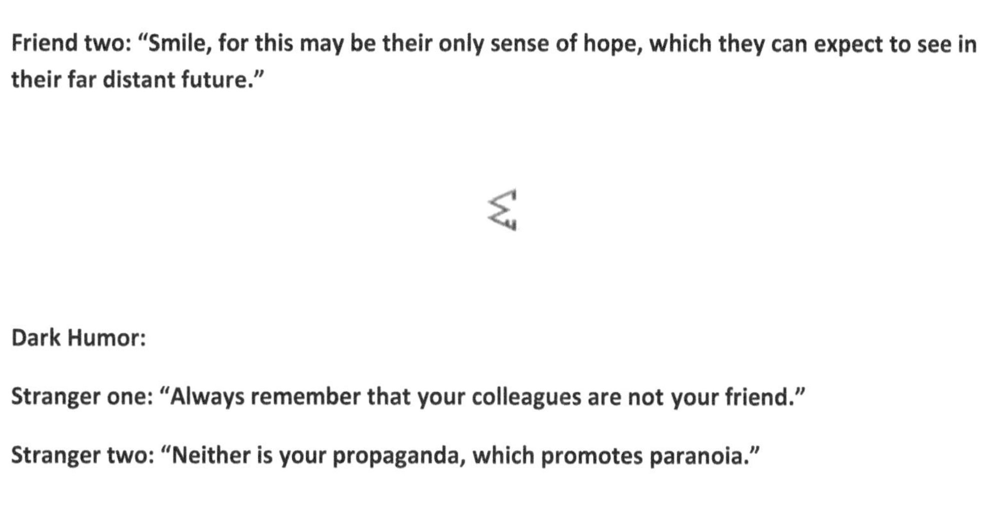

Dark Humor:

Stranger one: "Always remember that your colleagues are not your friend."

Stranger two: "Neither is your propaganda, which promotes paranoia."

Dark Humor:

Stranger one: "Why do you choose to revel in being a loner, versus chasing the beauty or desires of your dreams?"

Stranger two: "Because, I, instead, choose to be balanced; and not travel outside of myself, in order to chase that which can cause me to be fraught with the leverage of uncertainty."

Dark humor:

Stranger one: "Why do you not allow people to get too close to you?"

Stranger two: "To avoid having to travel an unfortunate distance within myself, in order to reestablish balance, should the circumstances become too volatile, precarious or uncertain by an onset of disharmony."

Dark Theological Humor:

Stranger one: "I believe in Jesus; for He was the perfect master, who saved me from all of my sins. So, why should I know you; for you have lived an abandoned, wild, adulterous and/or profligate life?"

Stranger two: "Because, "I AM" the last plea of the DIVINE Essence to save you from your existential undoing."

Stranger one: "How can you do that?"

Stranger two: "By offering the truth of love and understanding."

Stranger one: "Yeah, right, I know Jesus."

Stranger two: "If you truly did, we should not be having this conversation."

Dark Theological Humor:

Stranger one: "I feel that you are the devil and also a joke."

Stranger two: "Good, since, every joke should have a punch or a punchline, prepare to brace yourself for a shock."

Dark Humor:

Spouse one: "Baby, you are the essence of a true warrior; why did you allow that individual to disrespect you?"

Spouse two: "That was only a bravado, by which, they were attempting to save face, for they proved that they had long since been conquered, when they first felt threatened to response hostilely, once, they encountered the amicable grace of my psychological disposition."

Dark Humor:

Nihilist: "You are so foolish to believe in an afterlife; there is nothing but oblivion, once you leave this life."

Spiritualist: "As was the memory of my birth, so much so that my parents were one of the only few to recall such an event."

Dark Humor:

Spouse one: "Baby, what if you found me sitting romantically at a table with someone else?"

Spouse two: "I would humbly and politely ask to sit down with you both."

Spouse one: "Why?"

Spouse two: "In order to study the appeal that I may possibly lack, so that I may know how to preemptively and psychologically rid myself of desiring one in the future, who may have your similar mental disposition."

Spouse one: "How could you do this with such poise?"

Spouse two: "Simple, because I choose to always have the freedom to be nonattached to that which is not reciprocal."

Dark Humor:

Stranger one: "Why can you not win?"

Stranger two: "Because, I see no profit in competition."

Stranger one: "Why can you not be broken?"

Stranger two: "Because, I have learned to find peace within my life's brokenness."

Stranger one: "So, how can you profess to be whole?"

Stranger two: "Because, I stand unafraid to reveal the intricacy of each and every absolute part of who I AM."

Dark Humor:

Stranger one: "I am a world historian, thus, I seek only concrete evidence and facts; for there is nothing that I will believe, unless, it is substantially proven."

Stranger two: "By your propensity to be(lie)ve hearsay, you may not have the psychological skills to be an effective attorney, but, you could also make a great theologian, to prove what it means to possess faith beyond a reasonable doubt."

Queries of Life: Peering into the Psychological Mirror

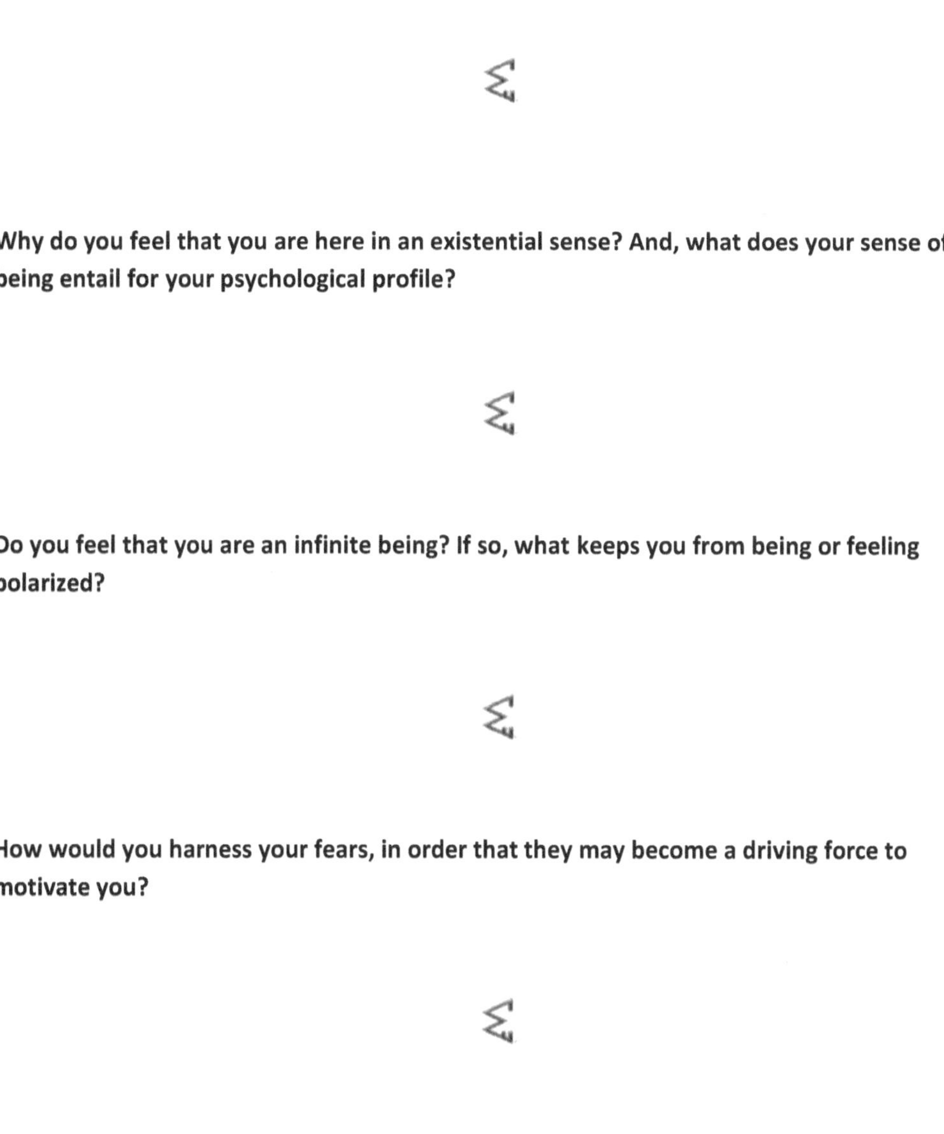

Why do you feel that you are here in an existential sense? And, what does your sense of being entail for your psychological profile?

Do you feel that you are an infinite being? If so, what keeps you from being or feeling polarized?

How would you harness your fears, in order that they may become a driving force to motivate you?

Could you humbly exert leadership at the costly price of being branded a servant?

Psychologically, do you feel that you have arrived?" If so, can you give a reasonable account of this destination?

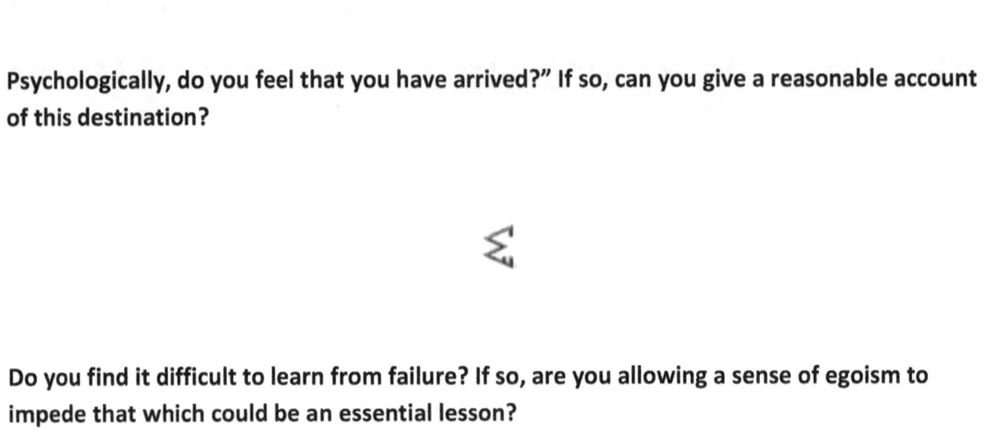

Do you find it difficult to learn from failure? If so, are you allowing a sense of egoism to impede that which could be an essential lesson?

Could you allow vanity to mask an authentic image of beauty, in order to fill a void of perceived ugliness?

Could you live with a convenient lie, even though you knew beforehand that it could cost you a lifetime of feeling barren of personal integrity?

Could you use hatred as a pretext to hide a total sense of love, in order to avoid the complications of feeling vulnerable to sincere expressions of affection?

If you knew that success would facilitate some of your greatest fears, would you still opt for the experience? If so, what would you do, in order to circumvent such possibilities?

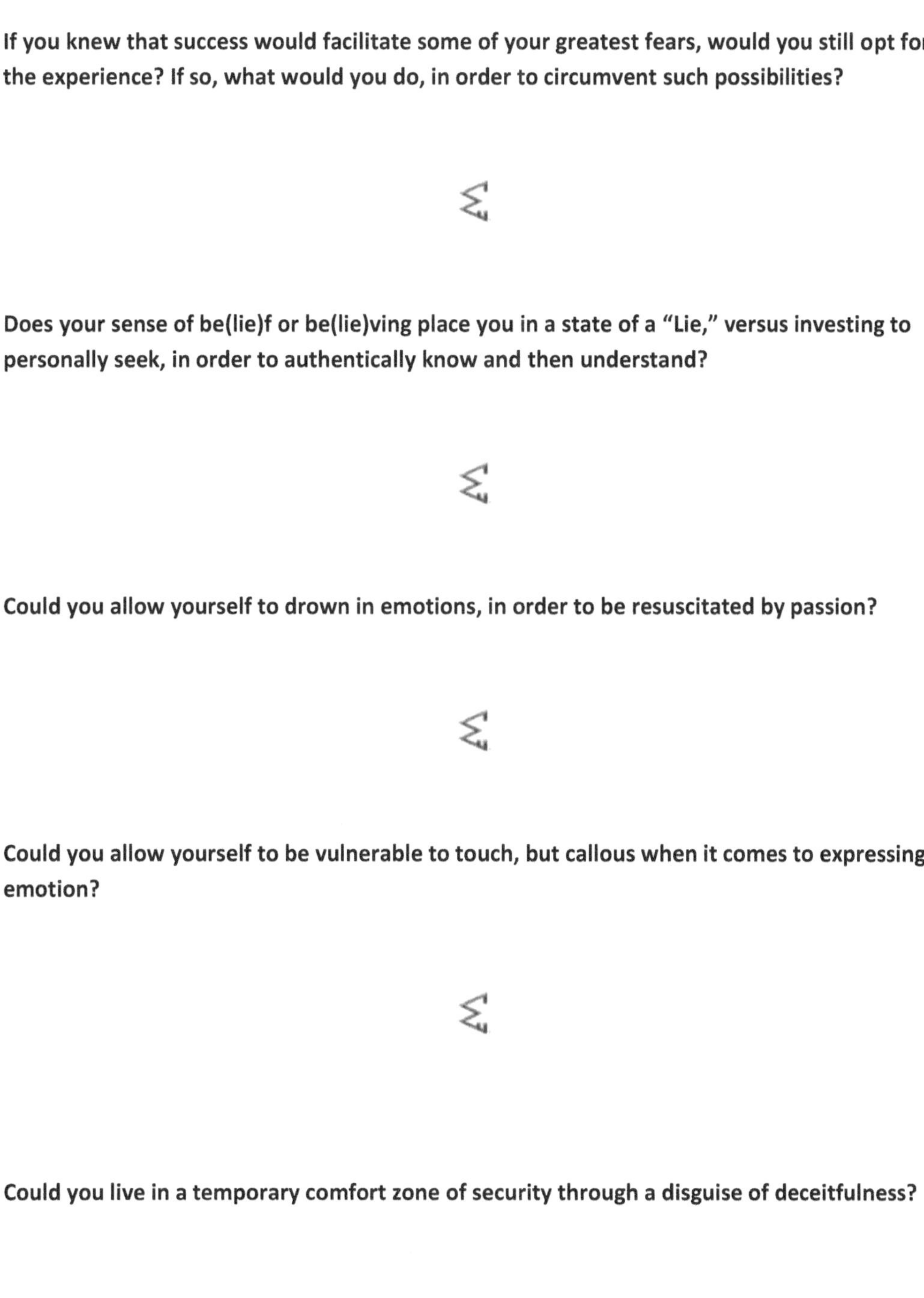

Does your sense of be(lie)f or be(lie)ving place you in a state of a "Lie," versus investing to personally seek, in order to authentically know and then understand?

Could you allow yourself to drown in emotions, in order to be resuscitated by passion?

Could you allow yourself to be vulnerable to touch, but callous when it comes to expressing emotion?

Could you live in a temporary comfort zone of security through a disguise of deceitfulness?

Could you enter a relationship with chances of knowing that it may fall apart, in order to find the missing pieces of who you truly are?

Could you entice another to reveal their worse aspects, in order that you may feel more of a sense of personal value?

Could you allow your sense of self-worth to become depreciated by a significant other's deliberate dismissal of attention?

Have you ever allowed yourself to accept the prevarications of others' opinion to become as a regarded fact?

Have you ever been willing to deceive yourself, in order to woo a convinced environment?

Could you drink or drug yourself into an oblivious state, in order to avoid a sobering truth?

Do you allow social conventions or fashions to impede your overall sense of personal dignity?

Could you make a lie feel comfortable by deliberately hiding the details of the truth?

Has a fear of openness or transparency caused you to develop a love for claustrophobic expression?

Could you ruthlessly deprive yourself of love, in order to willfully demonstrate the frozen quality or nature of your disinterested disposition, in an effort to prove that you can be a force of reckoning?

Do you find it quite easy to let go, for fear of holding on too tightly?

Does your sense of intimacy cause you to notice and enjoy certain details that others may find bothersome?

Could you find yourself devoting your time to an insubstantial assumption?

Could you say that you think that you have seen it all, at the inadvertent cost of being ignorant to that which you truly are or can further become?

Could you hold others' esteem of approval so highly that it causes you to jeopardize your own?

Do you vehemently speak of freedom, because of having a mentality that remains a captive of fear?

Do you ever find that you are eagerly ready to condemn others, in order to condone your personal discrepancies?

Do you find that when you gauge beauty solely from an external lens, you are, at times, internally repulsed by what you choose to see?

Are you masking yourself in a sense of benevolence, in order to hide a strong predilection for evil behavior?

Do you find that your apathy for personal improvement is sponsored by an indolence of seeking convenience and comfort?

Do you find that your sense of sanity is plagued by trying to uphold impractical expectations?

Do you feel that when you choose not to accept your psychological orientation, you become a victim of shallow or petty ideologies?

Do you find that you, at times, allow jealousy to paralyze your ability to be an authentic person?

Could you forfeit a moment of experiencing kindness, by maliciously continuing to savor the bitterness of a memory?

Do you, at times, find hope in witnessing the miseries of another's misfortune?

Could you find it troubling to have solutions to questions that others refuse to ask?

While within a social setting, could you humbly allow yourself to absorb what others can offer, without feeling the need to give unwelcomed knowledge?

Do you find yourself exceedingly empty; because you are full of unsustain desires?

Do you seek variety in your life, once you realize that you have become too bored with the usualness of yourself?

Could you find happiness in a state that would be disinclined to offer the bliss that you seek?

Do you realize that you are the greatest mystery, yet to be ever uncovered?

Closing Statement

As I conclude this eleventh book project, I AM compelled to say that I have become an apostate of be(lie)f or be(lie)ving, in much of anything. This includes the all-encompassing and all-pervading principle of existence-itself, which can be commonly referred to as GOD. For, I, in and of myself, know GOD; now, you may ask, how can you make such a bold assertion? My answer would be to encourage you to take a firm look into the psychological mirror of yourself, to see, as I have seen, the true psychogenic imprint of the absolute nature and/or quality of existence; in order to witness an indelible Oneness, which ever yearns to be acquainted with an inevitably harmonious union. So, to put it simply, if you seek GOD, endeavor to become ever acquainted with understanding the boundless quality of who you truly are; for here you will experience a psychological fullness, which cannot be discounted by insubstantial be(lie)fs and values of that which the mere identity of man/woman is always seeking, but is ever yet to find.